Minding Your Time

About the Author

David has spent nearly a quarter century studying his own introversion and learning to understand the strengths, gifts, and needs that are a part of being an introvert. David holds a Bachelor of Science in Psychology from Brigham Young University, as well as a Master of Education in Counseling from Northern Arizona University.

Professionally, David has worked in a variety of areas such as construction, retail, and higher education. He has also held many leadership positions and is a business owner. He enjoys presenting on the topics of personality and success and helping others work within their own strengths.

David resides in Arizona and loves spending time with his wife and three kids.

David hopes that through his work, introversion becomes better understood and embraced. *Minding Your Time* is the first in a series of books geared towards helping introverts find success.

Minding Your Time:

Time Management, Productivity, and Success, Especially for Introverts

DAVID HALL

ISBN: 9781976740817

Cover design © 2017 by TCS Design Group

I dedicate this book:

To my amazing and beautiful wife. She has helped make this book possible through her multiple talents and her never-ending belief in me.

To my three awesome kids, each brilliant in their own unique way. Now maybe they will stop asking, "Is your book done yet?"

To the many authors and speakers who help get the word out that introversion is not something to be fixed or cured, but rather needs to be understood, nurtured, supported, and celebrated.

Disclaimer

The book *Minding Your Time: Time Management, Productivity and Success, Especially for Introverts* is meant to help introverted people understand their own needs and strengths as it comes to time management, and learn to get the most out of their daily schedule. It could also serve as a reference for managers, employers, teachers, parents, and other supporters of introverts to help mentor them.

This book does not replace counseling, professional coaching, or therapy. The information and resources in this book are provided for informational and educational purposes only. There are several examples and case studies presented in this book, but the real names were replaced with fictitious ones to preserve confidentiality.

Whenever a gender-specific term was used, it should be understood as referring to both genders, unless explicitly stated. This is done solely for the purpose of making the text easier to read, and no offense or sexism is intended. Neither the author or the publisher can be held responsible for the use of the information provided within this book.

x

Contents

Don't miss our *FREE Bonus: MYT Workbook: 9 Strategies
To Better Time Management, Especially for Introverts*
at the end of the book.

ask yourself:
"are you satisfied
with your life?"

Introduction

I woke up early to have a few extra minutes to review my notes and ready myself for a presentation on personality, strengths, and introversion I was giving at a large women's conference. I was only one of two men presenting at the two-day event. I wasn't nervous because I've given similar presentations numerous times to a variety of groups. But as an introvert, I always like a little quiet time before going "on stage" for a presentation to gather my thoughts and recharge my mind. I know my strengths. I know my needs. I know what makes me be at my best.

Even though I'm usually racing from one thing to

the next (aren't we all?) and never truly have enough time, I've discovered some specific actions that I need to take to be more efficient, effective, and energetic. I'm getting more done than ever before.

Over the years, I've done quite a bit of reading on time management, productivity, and success to improve on my ability to get things accomplished. While always trying to get more done each day, I've discovered that some time management strategies work for me and some don't. At the same time, within the last few years, I've come to understand that I am an introvert. And, more than just recognizing that I am an introvert, I have come to realize that as an introvert, I have certain gifts and strengths that allow me to make unique and insightful contributions. I also have specific needs that I should be aware of. In my journey to better understand myself and my introversion, I have read many self-help books, and it's been my experience that extroverted solutions may not solve introverted issues. For example, if you are an introvert and want to get better at networking, you would be better served by reading a book on networking by a successful introvert that understands your strengths and needs. Following suggestions from an extroverted writer may lead to frustration and ineffectiveness, leaving the introvert feeling drained. Don't compare yourself to others that have different strengths. Rather, figure out what is true about you and work your strengths and needs into your strategies for success. While there are many great time management tips out there that may appeal to introverts, I haven't come across many time management tips specifically for introverts.

In my life-long study of introversion, I've learned how to focus my introverted mind to better manage my time. And in the chapters of this little book, I'll share what I've learned about minding your time so you can do it too.

Are you living the life you want?
If not, now is the time.

Do you feel like you have more to do than you have time for? This has been a problem for me over the years, as I always have a formidable amount of "to-do's" to get done both at work and at home. I've discovered that no matter how hard I work and how smart I work, there is ALWAYS more to do. I used to think, "If only I was more organized..." I have come to realize that just getting organized was not going to be enough, but rather it was important to use my specific strengths and also keep my particular needs in mind.

Introversion or extroversion is a significant part of one's personality, so it's crucial to be aware of your own unique strengths and needs when choosing and implementing strategies for time management and success. A major key to understanding and addressing your individual strengths and needs is to mind your time, that is, keeping your mind on track and focused on the tasks at hand. Some of the major things that I have learned that introverts need are as follows:

(1) **Time to clear your mind,**

(2) **Quiet focused time for certain tasks and projects,**

(3) **Time to prepare, plan, reflect, and think, and**

(4) **Time to recharge each day to be effective.**

As an introvert, I will always be thinking about and tweaking my time management system. I am not claiming to be perfect, but have greatly improved my time management skills by understanding what I need. I have some strategies to share that have made a difference in my life, and I hope you will find them helpful. I'll discuss each of these activities in the following chapters as well as share a few tips that I have found to be helpful in streamlining my workflow. Of course, I still have more to do than is humanly possible, but using these strategies has helped me become so much more productive than I ever was in the past.

While this book is geared toward the introvert, an extrovert could also benefit, either from general time management strategies or to better understand the introvert in their life – whether that be a spouse, child, brother, sister, student, co-worker, employee, boss, customer, or acquaintance.

Implementing these introvert-based strategies that work with your own gifts and allow you to fulfill your needs is key in being more organized. It is not a one-size-fits-all when it comes to time management, productivity, and success. What strategies will be effective for you? I know I am much happier and far more productive and successful than I've ever been simply by being true to myself and my strengths. As an introvert, understanding your own strengths and needs — and how to make the most of them — will be the secret to your success.

Understanding
Introversion

$$2$$

I've always been a deep thinker and, at times, I wasn't sure if this was a blessing or a curse. And having always had an inner push towards excellence, I was not always sure how to overcome my perceived weaknesses. I knew there was greatness inside of me, but couldn't understand why I didn't have this quality or that quality that I saw in others. I have been on a long journey to get to know myself and learn to be successful.

As Aristotle said, "Knowing yourself is the beginning of all wisdom."

For this reason, I have been studying psychology and observing people (including myself) for over 25 years now through university courses at the undergraduate and graduate level, in books, through Internet research, in seminars, at workshops, in webinars, and through countless hours of introspection and analysis, which, as an introvert, I am very good at! Through these years of struggle, I've had many epiphanies and have come to better understand myself and embrace the fact that I am an introvert.

One of these epiphanies came during a three-day professional development workshop. At the end of the three days, the facilitator spoke with me and told me that she was impressed with me. She told me that I was quiet and strong, and when I spoke, people listened. Yes, I can be considered "quiet" as I am often lost in thought. I may not have been as chatty as others in the workshop, but I had some valuable insights. The ability to go deep into thought is a gift as I often discover valuable insights that others might miss.

Introversion is so often misunderstood, and often the label has a negative connotation. For example, when I say "introvert," you might be thinking about someone who is shy, withdrawn from others, lacks self-confidence or is considered a loner. I know those are traits commonly associated with the word. In this book, I'll refer to the definition of the word by Carl Jung, who actually coined the term "introvert." According to Jung, introverts are those who are more focused inwardly on thoughts and ideas, whereas extroverts are more focused on the outer world.

As introverts, our minds have the ability to think deeply, and this is one of our greatest gifts. With the ability to think deeply comes much creativity, imagination, and innovation. Introverts tend to think through things before acting and can come up with some ingenious solutions and avoid problems. Many more things could be listed, but keep in mind not all introverts are alike. My purpose is not to say that introversion is better or extroversion is better, but rather that we all have unique gifts that need to be understood, nurtured, supported, and celebrated. Being introverted or extroverted is like being right or left handed. You don't choose introversion, but you can choose to embrace it. We are naturally wired in a certain way – either to process information internally or to process information externally.

None of us are exactly alike. Personalities are unique for each individual, and there are as many different personalities as there are people. Much of the current information I've reviewed seems to lump all introverts into one category – one size fits all. Since our personalities are multifaceted, a one size fits all isn't going to work for everyone. However, there are some commonalities that we can come to understand and appreciate from all sides of the introversion/extroversion spectrum.

Experts agree that 45-55% [CAPT.org] of the population are introverts, so either you are an introvert or you know someone who is. My work in this book and on my blog at quietandstrong.com is dedicated to helping people embrace their own introversion and to bring understanding to extroverts about the introverts in their lives. I hope to be able to help introverts (including myself) embrace their natural strengths and bring a greater understanding to all about introversion and extroversion.

So are you an introvert or extrovert? On the chart on the next page are some of the defining characteristics of introversion and extroversion that I have found helpful. Which side did you relate to the most?

Don't know if you are an introvert or extrovert? There are many great assessments such as the Myers-Briggs Type Indicator (MBTI) available online. The MBTI assessment also measures several other aspects of personality, so you can gain a better overall

introverts

□ naturally spend more time in their inner world of ideas.

□ think and then speak.

□ may prefer to communicate in writing rather than speaking.

□ may be drained by social interaction, but energized by time alone.

□ prefer deep conversations over small talk.

□ usually prefer a close circle of friends.

extroverts

□ naturally spend more time focused on the outer world around them.

□ speak to think.

□ may prefer to communicate by speaking rather than writing.

□ may be energized by social interaction, but may feel restless when experiencing excessive isolation.

□ in general enjoy most types of conversation.

□ enjoy having many friends and acquaintances.

picture of your introversion or extroversion. Keep in mind that personality assessments are a good tool for understanding yourself, but as you learn about yourself, don't get too hung up on the labels. Labels are simply a means of grouping characteristics for better understanding. They should never be used to limit or box in, and certainly, the label only applies as far as it is true for you. Please keep in mind that not all introverts are alike. Some introverts may have a strength for seeing the big picture, while others may excel at working with the details. Some introverts may be very logical and analytical, while others may be more in touch with their feelings and the feelings of others. Some introverts may be very organized and scheduled, while others may be more flexible and spontaneous. This list could go on.

Regardless of your personality type, whether you identify as an introvert (processing information internally), an extrovert (processing information externally), you have specific strengths and weaknesses. Find what's great about you, whether it's part of a label or not. In addition to assessments, there are many great books out there that can help. (I have listed a few on introversion in my recommended reading list at the end of this book). You could also attend workshops, work with a coach or counselor, read blogs (such as my blog at quietandstrong.com), and do some serious self-reflection, which introverts are particularly gifted.

Processing Internally Versus Externally

As I studied and learned about introversion, I've seen that introverts and extroverts have different communication styles and different strengths. Part of my definition of introversion is how much a person is naturally drawn to their inner world of ideas and how much this inner world is valued. You usually don't change whether you naturally focus on the outer world around you or your inner world of thoughts and ideas, but you can understand how your learning preferences and personality styles work. In doing this, you can learn to embrace your strengths.

I have had many epiphanies related to this, but one occurred when I was talking to a neighbor. We were talking about where we worked and it turned out his company is right across the street from mine. The funny thing was, when he told me the name of his company I did not recognize it. He was aware that my company was next to his, but I did not recognize the name of his company that I had driven by every day for a few years. This is because as I am driving, I am generally in my head thinking. This is so natural for me to drift into thought. I didn't choose it and I can't change it. Of course, I can focus on the outer world when needed, but my natural tendency to focus inward is a part of me. In speaking with and observing the extroverts around me they seem to be much more in tune with the outer world around them. Of course, we all do both, but what is your natural preference? Introversion and extroversion are not good or bad, they just are.

Thinking Before Speaking

I think! I think a lot and I usually think before I speak. The amount of time I spend thinking is not going to change for me, nor do I really want to change this. But understanding this about myself really takes away some limits and has helped me change how I interact with others.

Do you think before speaking as an introvert or do you speak to think as an extrovert would? Do you find yourself wondering, "Why is that person talking so fast and why am I struggling to keep up or get a word in?" I have learned that it is a natural process for me to put together my thoughts and then speak. Often extroverts speak in order to think or think out loud. Understanding these differences can greatly improve your communication with others.

For example, I was talking on the phone with a client and as she was just a little into telling me her story, she started saying, "Are you there? Are you there?" I, of course, assured her that I was listening to her. I have learned that, especially when talking to those that are uncomfortable with silence, it is necessary to tell people that I am listening from time to time, or throw in the occasional "OK." Also for those uncomfortable with silence, I need to tell them when I need a minute while looking up some information. I tend to not talk while I am doing this and this can also make some callers uneasy. Sometimes I actually ask to put them on hold if I think it will be a minute or so. In any conversation I have learned that sometimes I need to say "let me think about that." This could be for a few seconds or even the next day.

If you understand yourself and how you operate, you can prepare for various situations and come up with strategies for success, such as ways to improve communication. Extroverts can learn to pause sometimes in conversation or understand a little silence from the introvert is normal while they process their thoughts.

Time for Recharge

It is said that introverts get energy from time alone and extroverts get energy from people. I think this is oversimplifying the discussion of energy. I do think that introverts tend to need time alone to recharge after spending time focusing outward. In my case, it is not all people that cause energy drain, but rather certain people and situations. Extroverts may need to recharge after spending time alone with their thoughts; they recharge by being around others. The scale of introversion and extroversion is a continuum. One introvert might need more time alone than another, and one extrovert might be able to handle more alone time before needing to find company than another extrovert might. No two introverts are exactly alike, nor do they have precisely the same needs. The same is true for extroverts. The key is understanding what you need and how this fits into your time management strategy. The topic of recharge will be discussed in a later chapter. Understanding your need for recharge can help you better manage your energy levels.

Action Steps:

1) Do some further study into introversion and extroversion. Books, blogs, and articles can provide additional insight.

2) Perhaps take an assessment, such as the Myers-Briggs Type Indicator, and learn more about your personality.

3) Consider working with a coach or a counselor, if you feel additional help is needed.

The Introvert Difference

$$\boxed{3}$$

As I have more and more discussions about introversion, I am finding that many introverts don't identify with the term introversion. After all, aren't introverts shy, strange, or aloof? Of course, no matter the perception, these are not what makes one an introvert.

In our society, at least in the United States, extroverted traits tend to be celebrated and recognized, while introverted traits are oftentimes considered flaws or weaknesses. At work, our office environments may be more geared for those with more extroverted gifts, with open cubicles, loud conversation and distraction, but often no place for quiet concentration. At school, those who are quiet might seem to be forgotten by the rest. On television, movies, sporting events, and in our own social circles, the "BIG" personalities are celebrated while the more quiet personas play a supporting role or are even criticized. Even at home, introverts may be compared to more extroverted siblings or friends in a negative way. But as introverts we need to start recognizing and celebrating the gifts of introversion, and helping others understand how incredible they are.

When we are envious of the gifts of others, we may spend our time wallowing in self-pity instead of developing our own strengths. We tend to compare inner selves with the outward appearance we may see in others. As a result, we may have a difficult time seeing the incredible gifts we each possess. We might fail to see how we can use our own strengths for greatness rather than just wishing for someone else's gifts. Consider where you'd be without the incredible talents of introverts like Bill Gates, Mark Zuckerberg, and so many others, who have truly made the world a better place. The important thing is to be true to oneself and to learn what your strengths and needs are, so you know how to operate for your greatest success.

Introverted does not mean shy.

Sure, some introverts are "quiet" in social situations, but some are not. Some introverts have always been as social as they want to be. And for some introverts – like me – being more social can be learned. If you're in a situation where you're uncomfortable, you might be considered shy. And while it may be more common for introverts to feel uncomfortable in certain social situations, it's not accurate to describe a person's comfort in social interaction as introverted or extroverted behavior. Also, it's important to not judge how social a person is as they may be perfectly happy NOT going to a big party with a room full of strangers.

Introversion is not a measure of confidence (such as in the case of someone being shy), but it is a measure of whether we most naturally process information internally (introverts) or externally (extroverts).

When we misunderstand and avoid the term, we can miss out on all the wonderful gifts that come with being an introvert and the understanding of ourselves that is needed to be more efficient, effective, and fulfilled in our daily lives. I have learned that shyness – which can be a problem for both introverts and extroverts - can be overcome! You can absolutely become more confident by understanding and embracing your own unique gifts. But an introvert who is shy may need different strategies to gain confidence and overcome shyness than an extrovert, because they are different. As I mentioned, introversion is a natural way of being; it is not usually something that can change, meaning I will always be a deep thinker and a dreamer, regardless of how I interact in social situations.

The question is, "Are you satisfied with your life?" If you feel like you are as social as you WANT to be, even if your friends wish you were more social, then you may be perfectly satisfied and it's just your friends who are not. But if the answer is no, then you may need to gain to a better understanding of yourself and why you are unsatisfied. Do you have the close connections you crave? Do you need more recognition in your accomplishments? What specific parts of your life are you unsatisfied with? Understand what traits you can change and learn how to embrace the gifts that are unique to you.

Also, it's important to keep in mind that introverts can be very successful in anything they want to accomplish. Your introverted gifts can take you far! For example, many introverts are perfectly comfortable speaking or interacting in a large group. They may still need to recharge after spending time focusing on the external world, but it doesn't mean they cannot successfully interact with others. On the same note, there may be times when an extrovert is withdrawn, isolated and alone. Sometimes, this is harder on the extrovert, who draws energy from the external, because they have isolated themselves from others. Situations change. Confidence changes. Your ability and comfort level in any given setting can change.

Yes, as an introvert, you can and will focus on the outer world many times every day, and extroverts must spend some time focusing within. But whether your mind is naturally drawn inward or tends to focus more on the outer world and how you are energized is always going a part of who you are. Learning to work with how your mind is naturally wired will help you become better able to manage situations where you do have to focus outward and understand how to be the best "you" you can be.

Some introverts are not getting what they want out of life because they lack an understanding of their introverted nature. This was me. For example, I didn't understand that a little time alone each day was a need. I didn't recognize that I have unique gifts that I needed to share and that it was not helpful to compare myself to others that have different strengths than me.

It's sometimes hard to stop comparing yourself to others, but you need to figure out what you want out of life. If you are happy, don't let others tell you that you're not. If you want more out of life, then get to know your strengths and needs and use those to get better! You generally won't change whether you are introverted or extroverted because that is a natural part of who you are, but you can come to a beautiful understanding of yourself and others to get everything you want out of life.

I recently gave a presentation that included a discussion of introversion and extroversion. After the presentation, a person I know well who was in the audience came up to talk to me. She said that even though she didn't really learn anything new, as she had studied the topic extensively, it was a great reminder that she was "OK." She told me that she was married to her best friend and they loved spending time together, just the two of them. She is social with others, but often feels pressure to spend more time socializing than she prefers.

Our discussion on introversion served as a reminder that she knows what she enjoys better than anyone else, and that it is OK to feel this way. Another person approached me and let me know that the presentation was very helpful and that she had no idea that she was an "introvert." From the presentation, she was able to get some insights into her introverted nature that she had not considered before. We need to have many more conversations on the unique gifts, strengths, and needs of both introverts and extroverts.

As I have gotten to know myself better, I have come up with a list of some needs and strengths I keep in mind as I make plans and set goals for myself. If you are a fellow introvert, you probably will have some similarities and also some differences to my list below. What will you add to your own list? Is there a statement

My Needs and Strengths

- I am only strong when I **understand** who I am and what I need.

- Quiet does not mean shy. Quiet for me means thinking before speaking, taking time to reflect, and getting lost in deep thought from time to time. **Quiet is a gift.**

- I usually need to think before speaking.

- I need to let people know when I need time to think.

- I need to set aside some alone time each day, whether at home or work, for reflection and recharge.

- I need to act according to **my values** and not worry what people think.

- There are some things about myself that I cannot change, such as the way I spend a lot of time in deep thought, but there are **many things I CAN change,** such as my thoughts around irrational fears.

- I can engage in small talk when I want to or need to, but it is fine if I avoid some.

- I need to work to make connections with everyone in my life.

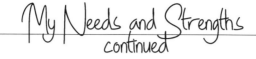

My Needs and Strengths
continued

- It takes work to deepen the close relationships I have, and it is worth it.

- I need to prepare for presentations and meetings as appropriate to minimize on-the-spot time to think.

- I need to remember to make my intentions, plans, and vision known to others and not assume they understand what is so clear in my head.

- I am a master at reflection and can use this ability to be better each day. I benefit greatly by reading the words of others and reflecting on them.

- I need to let my voice be heard, whether in person or through writing.

- I need to strive to have focus as I work on important and meaningful projects. Multitasking is not usually effective for me.

- I remember that everyone has great gifts, **including me.** I will be my very best and only compare to myself and not others.

I will dream big and act on my dreams.

WHY NOT ME?

below that you do not relate to? Again, no introvert or extrovert is exactly alike, so your list may different than mine.

Embracing Introversion

As I mentioned earlier, being an introvert or extrovert is not good or bad, but it is the way you are wired and is your natural way of being. It's been my experience that as I have come to understand myself and my introverted traits — such as the fact that I think deeply, usually think before speaking, sometimes need some alone time, and prefer deep conversations versus small talk — that I no longer feel that I am being "held back" by limitations or paralyzed by fear. For years, I tried to "learn" to be an extrovert. What I didn't understand was that what I perceived as flaws, were, in reality, some of my greatest strengths. Working with my natural gifts instead of against them, I have become so much more successful than ever before.

Embracing introversion is not about making any excuses for not being my best or getting everything I want out of life. I have learned that if I want to be successful, I need to figure out what makes me strong and how I can be my best as an introvert.

Action Steps:

1) Think about your unique strengths. Write down as many as you can think of, and identify how they can help you.

2) Think about your own needs – whether it be needing time to think, needing to recharge, or whatever needs are unique to you. Understanding and meeting these needs will be key to increasing your effectiveness.

Focus on the Important

4

Rory Vaden, in *Procrastinate on Purpose*, states:

"Success in business, at home and in life doesn't come from applying our resources proportionately throughout different areas. In fact, it's just the opposite. Success usually is the result of focusing our talents, money, time or energy in one priority direction for a shorter period of time to create a desired result, which in Take the Stairs (another book by Vaden) I called a 'season.' In one word a season is best defined as 'imbalance'."

I am realizing that, when trying to do it all, I feel out of control and that I'm not accomplishing some of things that are most important to me. In order to be successful, you need to decide what your top priorities are. I like how Vaden categorizes the various areas of life: faith, family, fitness, fun, faculty (work), and finances. What are my most important priorities in each of these areas? What goals will I accomplish and what will I leave undone? Realizing your goals is not about checking a lot of to-do's off of a list, but instead deciding what is truly most important to you, identifying what activities you should do to achieve your goals, and then putting those activities into action. I have also come to learn that success is not about balance, but about priorities. Some days you may need to spend more time on a particular project or some days you may need more of a break alone or with your family.

Success is not about balance, but about priorities.

I came to a point recently in both my work and home life where I was feeling so overwhelmed. I was spending too much time at work, not enough time at home, and just feeling like I was "spinning my wheels." I made a list of my top three projects that I needed to accomplish this coming year at work. I listed my various roles in life (husband, father, brother, supervisor, employee, etc.) and the various areas of faith, family, fitness, fun, faculty (work), and finances. I made a visual of my top priorities and refer to it when I am getting caught up in the day to day work, activities, and other "fires," so I don't lose sight of what is most important.

From time to time, you need to find a quiet place to give your most important priorities some serious thought. As an introvert, you have a great gift of reflection, but you have to give yourself some time and have a space for some deep thought. What are the major things you want to accomplish? What are some short-term goals? What are some long-term goals? What are the big lifetime goals you want to accomplish? What are the day-to-day things you need to do? What do you want to do? What does an ideal day look like for you? What do you need to stop doing?

An example for me has been writing this book. I have been working on it, but not nearly enough. Completing this book has been a huge goal of mine for this past year, and in order to achieve it, I needed to find far more time, focus, and "imbalance" than I thought was available. I needed to make a plan of how I would accomplish this. I had to decide what it would take each day and each week to accomplish my goal. I had to set a timeline and determine when I wanted to be finished. Over and over, I have heard that you need to carve out a regular time to write, and often this is daily. I had to look to experts in the field and determine whether there were others that I could learn from. In this case, there are many authors out there that share their stories, so I spent time learning from those I respected. I was able to use some of their expertise and incorporate it to find the resources needed to finally get this book completed.

What are your most significant goals and what will you need to do to accomplish them?

Action Steps:

1) Take some time to identify what's important in your life, and where you should focus your time and energy.

   a. Identify your roles and responsibilities, and what things MUST be done.

   b. Identify your goals and aspirations, and what things you have a great DESIRE to do.

   c. Identify where your focus needs to be, and recognize that you will need to have imbalance sometimes to succeed in your goals.

2) Identify the things that are keeping you from success.

   a. Is there something you can assign or pass off to someone else to free up your time?

   b. Is there something you can let go of to make time for other things?

   c. Are there activities you can streamline or spend less time doing, to give you more time to spend on the important activities you identified in step one?

3) Focus on the important.

   a. Set a timeline and create action steps you must take to complete your goal.

   b. Determine a specific time or times that you will focus on the action steps you created in part 3a above.

   c. Determine if there are other experts who can help – whether by learning from their works, or having them as a mentor.

   d. Get it DONE!

Time to Recharge

$$5$$

The concept of an introvert's need for recharge is well known. But with so many different types of introverts, the need for recharge is not the same for everyone. The important thing is to know yourself and what you need. Once you know what it is you need, you can build it into your weekly plan.

I am not an introvert because I need to recharge. I need to recharge BECAUSE I'm an introvert. Being a deep thinker is what is at the heart of my introversion. I turn inward to thought more often than not. This is how I naturally process the world around me – internally rather than externally. So, when I'm spending more time focused externally, this tends to drain my energy.

Other introverts may be more in tune with their feelings and the feelings of others. This type of introvert might experience a drain caused by the overwhelming sense of the feelings of others. The important idea here is that you need to understand what causes your energy to drain, and then build in time for recharge as needed to stay energized and at the top of your game.

I was thinking about my own energy levels as I had a series of small group discussions with members of a large team recently. This team meets regularly as a large group, but with so many team members, not everyone gets a chance to speak. The smaller group sessions allow for all to participate, and we had some great discussions as a result.

After facilitating three of these in a row, I realized I was feeling quite drained. Often, I associate this drain with something that I do not enjoy, such as mindless small talk or networking with strangers. But in this case, I was having great discussions about important topics. I realized that my energy drain is not necessarily caused by things that are unpleasant to me. So, what do I do when something I like doing leaves me feeling drained? In this case, I was able to schedule a break right after.

My days are never the same, so I just do my best to not schedule draining activities back-to-back whenever possible. Sometimes, I am able to plan my schedule, but often my schedule is determined by others. On days I find myself in consecutive activities and back-to-back meetings that drain me, I have to find other strategies to keep up my energy until I can recharge.

One particular day was jam-packed with meetings where I was either in charge of the meeting or was an important contributing member of the meeting. The meetings were filled with decisions that needed to be made and many variables and situations that needed to be worked out. It involved quite a bit of back and forth with my colleagues. As I mentioned, some days like this could be draining, but this day I was energized by thinking through problems and coming up with solutions in a collaborative way. So, to me, not every meeting is draining in the same way. The key for me has been getting to know myself, so I can anticipate which activities will be draining, and planning when I will need a break.

In general, if I am able, I schedule a little space in between meetings. I may still be doing some work, but I at least have some alone time to recharge. Sometimes meetings are back-to-back without a break. Maybe I can get a little recharge on the walk between meetings. But sometimes there is no relief during the workday. On these days, I can adjust my thoughts to cope until there is recharge time. Sometimes this recharge might have to wait until the drive home. The drive home is one of my big recharge times... Just me and my thoughts and maybe a little music.

In planning your schedule and maintaining energy for all the "external processing" activities you'll encounter during the day, the first step is recognizing those activities that tend to drain you. If you have to give a presentation or lead a meeting and you know that "being on stage" wears you out, you might try to arrange your schedule so you have some time alone to reflect afterward.

Understand what drains you, and when you need a recharge.

When you are not able to fully arrange your schedule, at least allow yourself breaks during the day if possible. For instance, take advantage of your commute times, and maybe find time later in the evening or early in the morning that you can use to focus and recharge each day. On the flip side of that, an extrovert may need some visiting/interacting time with others to recharge after spending time working alone on a task or project. Introverts are not the only ones who need recharge.

Extroverts may feel restless or trapped when they spend excessive time alone — they might recharge by visiting with others in the office, or needing other social activities that would drain an introvert. Everyone is different. When you begin to understand what drains you and what types of recharge work best, you can better maintain your energy focus.

It's often said that people drain introverts. For me, I found that not all people drain me, but certain people and situations do. I spent an afternoon hanging out with some of my favorite people in the world, my siblings. In this case I was not drained, but quite the opposite. I was energized by the conversation. It was great to talk about the good old days, some of the crazy things that happened to us as kids, what we are doing now, and what big plans we have for the future. Draining? Quite the opposite.

In *The Introvert's Way*, Sophia Dembling says "...I could make a case that introverts are more genuinely people-oriented than extroverts because we're always on the lookout for connections and conversations, whereas extroverts are content with noise and chatter." That's it... I don't enjoy the noise and chatter! So, I won't feel guilty about not enjoying the noise and chatter or apologize for not enjoying it.

I can get drained by noisy environments if I am trying to carry on conversations. However, noisy environments do not always drain me. One vacation day, I spent ten hours at an indoor amusement park with my kids – video games, go-karts, bumper cars, mini roller coasters, etc. There were a lot people there since many kids were out of school. My kids had a great time and they were not tired until the place was closing. I had a great time too.

This event started me thinking about the various opinions I have been reading about introverts and the need for recharge. That day, I had a great time the entire day and did not feel the need to be "alone." I love my kids and love spending time with them. So for me, neither the crowd of people nor lots of noise or other activities going on around me triggered the need for alone time and recharge.

I'm sure there are some introverts out there that

could have experienced a similar day as I did with the crowds and activity and would definitely need the alone time to recharge after. Introverts are each different and experience the world differently. The important thing is to know yourself and what YOU need.

I think too many people try to put introverts neatly into a box, but this doesn't work. You need to understand how you best operate and plan for recharge as much as you can, so you can be your best, most productive, and happy self.

The introvert "need for recharge" is a real thing. Introverts, when able to fulfill this need, will be more successful and productive. Many say that extroverts get energy through people-interaction and introverts need some solitude away from people, because, in fact, it is people that are draining the introvert's energy. In my opinion, an introvert's desire to be alone and recharge is truly just the result of the energy drain caused by shifting one's focus onto the external, instead of the introvert's natural internal processing.

For me, it is not people in general that drain me or give me the need to recharge, but rather situations requiring external focus that cause strain in my thinking. For example, with people who talk a lot – it's not the person that is draining, but the continual talking that doesn't allow an introvert to think. Or when networking or "working a room" it's not the people in the room that are draining, but the need to get outside one's own mind to carry on small talk that causes the drain.

Here are a few things that trigger the recharge need for me:

- When I am trying to think and because of interruptions or too many things happening, I can't. Again, thinking for introverts is very natural, but in certain environments, not being able to process your thoughts can be very draining.

- Strained conversation with strangers or those I don't relate to very well. For me, it's not people in general that drain me, but certain people and certain situations.

- Being "on stage" as the center of attention or extended periods of time. For me, some examples of this would be running meetings, attending meetings, giving presentations, or conducting training.

What triggers your need to recharge? And once you've determined what causes you to be drained, how do you make time to recharge? For example, can you block out some time right after that meeting or situation that drained you? When I schedule a little time for recharge, I'm better able to function after a draining situation. Once again, I don't think all introverts fit neatly into a box, but it's important to get to know ourselves, understand how we function best, and learn what drains and recharges us, so as much as possible, we can build recharge opportunities into our daily routine to maintain our energy throughout the day.

In addition to the daily recharge, I have found that a longer-term recharge from time to time is very beneficial.

In *Introvert Power*, Dr. Laurie Helgoe has an entire chapter devoted to taking a retreat.

"As the term implies, a retreat is a backing away, a withdrawal, an experience in the realm of yin, an act of introversion. A retreat can be a ten-minute break or an extended escape – such as Paul Gauguin's two-year artistic sabbatical in Tahiti – but we usually think of a retreat as a weekend or vacation-length trip "away from it all." For an introvert, retreating is the ultimate indulgence: an inner life binge that fills our depleted energy stores." Dr. Helgoe gives many examples and suggestions for retreats, including a trip to a Bed &

Breakfast she took alone.

Taking a vacation without my wife and kids? Am I allowed to do this? Probably not. I usually go to a work conference a couple of times a year, and often, if I can have some time to myself it does have a wonderful retreat-like effect. When I have the opportunity to enjoy periods of solitude, I get some needed peace back in my life. It gives me time to put things into perspective or to reflect on my life's dreams. However, up until recently, I did not fully realize that this solitude was a must for me and not an option if I was going to be happy and successful. One of the major keys to success and happiness is knowing how you operate best and what you need.

On a recent holiday weekend, I stayed home from a family outing. This is not something that I usually do. However, coming off of a very busy time at work and looking ahead to my upcoming busy schedule, I knew that I needed it. A "day off" alone was what I needed at the time and my family did have fun without me. This is not something I plan to do often, as I love my family and love spending time with them. However, in this case it was the right thing to do. The time home alone was just what I needed and very good for my soul.

I believe that some of our greatest happiness comes from serving others. However, it is very important that we take time to take care of ourselves so that we can actually serve others better. I like the way Steve Chandler puts it in his book, *Fearless*:

"It takes courage to put yourself first. We've been shamed for being selfish. That was always the most cutting accusation. But when you start honoring your own time with yourself, you will still serve others. In fact even better. Because there's a more focused, masterful you to do the serving. So the difference is this: your own life comes first: a fearless decision."

In our busy lives, sometimes we feel guilty or get guilt from others when we need to take time for ourselves. We have to remember that if we don't take care of ourselves, we won't be nearly as effective at taking care of anyone else. But when we are fully charged we will have what it takes to take on the many responsibilities and challenges we face daily.

You will need extended breaks from time to time. Don't feel guilty about it. I was thinking about this on a family vacation. The vacation was over a holiday weekend. We were hanging out with our extended family in the mountains. It was fun to catch up with my siblings and enjoy the beautiful surroundings. Although I really did enjoy traveling and seeing everyone, it was not all that relaxing to me. I'm at a point in my life where I try to take at least one day off work at home before I travel and one day off after I return home. These days off at home are what are truly relaxing to me.

After we returned home, I took off a few extra days after our trip. It was nice to have a little more time off; however, I still had plenty to do at home too. I found my mind wanting to take a little more vacation, but I was feeling guilty for not constantly getting things done. I often can't help but to think about what I need to do at work, at home, for my blog, and so many other things.

But this vacation, while I still did plenty of thinking about the usual concerns, I decided to give my mind a much needed break. I spent a little time letting my mind just wander. I enjoyed the mind-break, but with so much to do, and so much going on at my work, I still felt a little guilty. Shouldn't I be doing something productive? As I learn more about being more effective, I am discovering that not only do I need some alone time to do my day-to-day work, I also need some time to relax. This relaxation is good for my mind and I should not feel guilty about it. I find I am ready to start the work week more refreshed after some travel, some down time at home, and a little down time for my mind. Introverts, don't feel guilty about letting your mind take a break. It may just be the medicine you need!

I am also a big fan of sometimes taking a week off and staying home or taking a staycation. This can actually be very relaxing for me as an introvert. Often when talking about taking a staycation, people ask "where are you going?" and I say "nowhere." I get puzzled looks and sometimes even looks of pity. I had a co-worker once who would never take vacation time if she was not going somewhere. It's funny that somehow our society in general thinks that you have to go somewhere to take vacation. I do like to travel, but my introverted self enjoys some time off work at home from time to time. This is a very healthy approach for me.

As an introvert, you need to allow yourself that time to recharge, to read a book, to exercise, to think — and whether you do that at home or while on a getaway, it's an important part of recharging and renewing your energy. You are not being selfish. You are taking care of yourself.

Action Steps:

1) Identify activities and situations that cause you to feel drained (meetings, social/networking situations, etc.)

2) Identify activities and situations that help you recharge (time alone to think, working on a different project, changing focus, quiet time, etc.)

3) Whenever possible, schedule time for recharging activities after draining activities.

4) Plan a personal retreat, quiet getaway, or staycation filled with recharging activities and allow yourself to take a brain break to fully recharge on a regular basis.

Balance of Quiet

6

I have discovered that as an introvert, I need some alone time. It can be hard to find this time with a busy family and work life. I woke up early one morning to enjoy some solitude and not long after, my young daughter woke up looking for some company. My daughter needs constant attention and most of the time, I love spending time with her. However, she does not understand when daddy (or mommy) needs just a little space. We hung out and watched a little TV and played a game. And then I slipped away for a bit more solitude.

My entire life, I have enjoyed solitude, but it has just been within the last few years I have realized it is a need, a need in my personal life and in my work life. I don't need or want solitude all day long, but a little time alone each day is how I work best. Sometimes, it's difficult to explain to your family that you need a little time alone and this is not a rejection of them, but rather a need to spend some time alone with your thoughts to rejuvenate and recharge.

Quiet Time at Home

It's funny that I have been married for many years and until I started writing about introversion, I didn't realize that not only do I need some solitude, but my introverted wife does too. I didn't realize this was why she was staying up later than the rest of the family, to have some peace and get some work done. Sometimes, to help her have quiet time, I take all the kids out of the house for the day and give her some time to herself.

Normally, we both put the kids to bed, but she understands every once in awhile, after a particularly long day at work that I need some space and she'll put the kids to bed so I can have alone time. Understanding each other's needs for solitude has been helpful. It is not perfect; I may need her company when she would like to be alone or the other way around, but either way, the understanding goes along way.

Quiet Time at Work

It can be a struggle at work to find time to be alone. Does everyone at your company expect you to have an "open door" policy? Do you need to be available to everyone at all times? I have learned that it's important for me to have solitude at work from time to time. Sometimes I go in to work earlier than everyone else to give myself quiet time at the office.

Going in early is not always possible, nor does it always provide enough time alone. So I do need to close my door on occasion. Again, this may appear as rejection to some, but I have found it necessary and helpful to communicate what I am doing. I might say, "I am in right now, but I am going to close my door while I work on..." so they better understand why my door is closed.

As introverts, we must continue to get the word out that there is a need for solitude in many of us, and that is not selfish or strange, but in reality, brings us to our best self. We think, and we think a lot, and sometimes with all that is happening we can get overwhelmed. From time to time we need to clear our minds.

This may take the form of a long walk or quietly sitting or any number of different activities. I've learned quite a bit about managing my time and energy to be more efficient over the years, but sometimes find it challenging to make time for myself to clear my mind, while balancing all of my other responsibilities.

I now know that not only do we do our best work when we have some time here and there to think, but as introverts, if we don't take time to clear our minds, overwhelm will set in. I have experienced being overwhelmed as I always have more to do than I have time for, but taking some quiet time here and there is well worth it even when you are very busy.

Managing my time while making time for myself is an ongoing struggle. I often spend a Saturday in the office when I have an important project or am just feeling overwhelmed. The office is closed Saturday, so I am normally all alone and it is nice and quiet. One particular Saturday, I went in to do a project that was very important, but hadn't been able to get to it in my day-to-day work, because there always seemed to be more pressing matters.

I have gone to work on many Saturdays (against my wife's will), but this time was a little different. Normally, when I go in on a Saturday, I am getting organized after a chaotic week or going in to finish up several small odd projects. This time I spent the entire day on this ONE project. I was extremely focused on the high level of detail that was required. I knew it was going to take several uninterrupted hours to complete.

So, if it took a full day of concentration which I normally don't have, how in the world was I going to finish during the busy work week, in-between everything else going on during a regular day? It seems that on a Saturday I am far more productive than I am on a normal weekday, when I have constant interruptions. But going in on Saturday is not the best strategy either, as I do have a family and a life outside of work.

I know that positions and workplaces vary. Some people work in offices that already recognize the need for quiet concentration, and some do not. I have learned to recognize my own need for quiet to accomplish certain tasks, so I close my door from time to time. But, I can't just close my door with total concentration for a whole day like I did on that Saturday. Don't get me wrong... aside from giving up my Saturday, I loved the full day of peace and quiet, but I would be bored with this level of solitude all of the time.

What about the people with no door? And no option or desire to go to work on a day off? I realize not everyone has a door or a quiet workspace. I have been without one plenty in my work life. But there are still some ways you can create a productive work environment for yourself.

Laura Stack in her book, *What To Do When There's Too Much To Do,* has some recommendations for those without a door and many will apply to those with a door as well:

- Turn your workspace away from active areas like busy hallways.

- Listen to soothing music or ambient noise to drown out incidental sounds.

- Wear noise-canceling or noise-attenuating earphones while you do the above. People might think you're listening to something and might be less likely to interrupt you.

- Set up a signal to let people know you need to work uninterrupted. For example, you might wear a red cap when you're deep into something and need to concentrate.

- Set a symbolic barrier across your doorway such as police tape or a cube door.

- Hold off responding to emails; close your email program to give yourself some time to focus.

- Send your calls directly to voicemail, so the ringing doesn't distract you.

- Turn off your cell phone (don't just set it to vibrate).

The above strategies are great advice. You may not be able to do all of the steps listed above, but you can select those strategies that will help you be most productive and focus on implementing those. You may need to do some convincing to get your managers and co-workers to cooperate.

You may meet some resistance to your new plan, but I do know as introverts we work better with some uninterrupted quiet time. As an introvert, you need some time to focus, especially when it comes to complex tasks and projects.

Do you know how much focused time you need each day? How much time do you need to interact with your team and those in your organization? The reality is that this quiet and focused time will make you more responsive to your team and your organization.

With a balance of quiet, we can get some great things accomplished. The social aspect is important for creating a "team" atmosphere and building relationships among co-workers. We introverts really do like people and social interaction. But, the quiet solitude is important for our concentration, analysis and deep thought.

Our workplaces need to recognize the strengths of each individual employee and provide balance between social and quiet time. What is your workplace culture? Does it support your needs for both collaborative time and solitude to focus? As an introvert, what strategies are you using to achieve this balance? Find a balance that makes you strong!

In the quiet, we can find focus. I know people that are very proud of their ability to multitask. However, as an introvert, multitasking does not work well for me. Honestly, I believe multitasking doesn't really work well for anyone. Stopping and starting and stopping and starting makes it harder to complete any project.

I find that I work best and am most efficient when I can focus on one project at a time. Of course, this approach isn't always an option. As busy people, we will usually be juggling many things, but to me, especially as an introvert, time to focus is the ideal.

The truth is that everyone functions better with less multitasking. We can truly only pay attention to one thing at a time. According to Dr. John Medina in *Brain Rules*:

"Studies show that a person who is interrupted takes 50 percent longer to accomplish a task. Not only that, he or she makes up to 50 percent more errors."

Instead of multitasking, Dr. Medina calls it "task-switching." Since people can only have one thought at a time, in order to attempt to do multiple things at the same time, they switch back and forth between thoughts. Some people are better at task-switching than others, but no one actually has the ability to think about more than one thing at a time.

A good share of my work day involves trying to answer emails, while the phone is ringing, someone shows up unexpectedly in my doorway with a problem, and there is a project (or three) in the background that is due soon. Personally, I am making efforts to get some quiet time in each day so I can focus on one task at a time.

I think that in addition to finding our own time to

focus, we also need to admit that multitasking is not effective in our work teams and we should try to arrange schedules such that each person on the team has some time to work without interruption on the projects he or she needs to accomplish. Let's stop talking about getting better at multitasking, and get better at getting work done.

Action Steps:

1) Try to block time in your schedule to focus on specific projects you need to complete.

2) Identify the projects that need quiet focus to complete.

3) Does your work culture and facility allow for quiet focus? If so, dedicate some quiet time to accomplish your projects. If you don't have a quiet space to work, inquire about using a small conference room with a door or other private space to get the project completed.

4) Minimize distractions in your workspace so that you can focus on the items that you need to work on. Turning off items of distraction (cell phone, email & other notifications) while you focus on your work

can help you to accomplish your tasks and be more efficient.

6) Although multitasking or "task-switching" is necessary in certain situations, try to complete each task before stopping and starting the next thing to be more effective in accomplishing your day-to-day activities.

Avoiding Overwhelm

$$\boxed{7}$$

Recently a colleague had been extremely stressed with the amount of work he had to do. "The emails never end, these deadlines are too tight, and there is no way to get all of my work done." Listening to him started stressing me out. Of course, I could have said the same about my work. I also have an endless amount of work and although I am better organized and work smarter than I used to, I still can't do it all. The difference is I have learned to change the messages and stories I tell myself.

If you are feeling overwhelmed, what thoughts are causing these feelings? Can you change your thoughts? I have an undoable amount of work and could easily get overwhelmed, but I choose to be realistic about the tasks before me. I get organized, prioritize, and recognize that I can only focus on the task at hand. I sometimes have to remind myself that getting overwhelmed really only slows me down. By changing the messages I send myself, I spend less time being worried about what I can't get done, and more time doing what I can. I still can't get everything done (as I have more to do than is humanly possible), but I am much more successful and effective when I choose not to be overwhelmed.

I have been trying for some time to get my workload under control. I have tweaked my system for organization over and over and have greatly improved my ability to get things done. Even as streamlined as I've made my workflow, I still have more to do than can ever be done. Too often I hear, "Did you get my email?" or "Is the project finished yet?" Some days I can go into work earlier, but some days my kids' school schedules or other activities prevent me from getting in any earlier than I do. I often stay late, but my goal is to be home for dinner every evening, as my kids are growing up way too fast. There simply are not enough hours in the day, and it would be very easy to become so overwhelmed as to not accomplish anything.

One strategy for avoiding overwhelm is to make a regular daily appointment with yourself at the beginning of the day, every single day. As an introvert, I find that a little uninterrupted time goes a long way. Ideally, I will spend this quiet time each morning and strategically identify my priorities for the day or week, organize my schedule, and work on those specific projects that require focus. Why haven't I done this before? Being available to everyone at all times is the culture that most of us live in. But, after many years (and late nights and Saturdays) I realize that, especially as an introvert, I need some "alone time" regularly to be productive. I still put in some late nights and Saturdays, but am working to make this much more of an exception.

Also, I want to clarify that prioritizing your activities is different than having a to-do list. My to-do list is endless, and would overwhelm anyone... probably much like your to-do list. However, I've found that by prioritizing the tasks that either have an eminent deadline, or are critical in some other way, I can focus on accomplishing the things that must be done in the time I have to do them. I also try to leave some time in my day for the emergencies that arise, and other interruptions and distractions that inevitably arise. And as I have additional time, I can focus on the less urgent tasks, but either way I am able to finish the most important tasks each day.

Figure out what steps and strategies you can use to create the quiet time you need to focus and avoid feeling overwhelmed. You'll be more productive, more successful, and less drained.

Action Steps:

1) Write down the thoughts you have that are leading to overwhelm. Then, on a separate piece of paper, write down possible alternative thoughts you could replace the overwhelming thoughts with. When a negative thought comes to mind, pull out your positive thought list and read those instead. Change the message that you are sending to yourself.

2) Make an appointment with yourself each day to have some quiet time to reflect, work and prioritize your day.

3) Write down your daily to-do list, and then prioritize it. Start with the most urgent task and then move on to subsequent tasks based on your prioritized list. This way, even if you don't accomplish everything, at least you are taking care of the most important items.

Managing Ideas

$$\boxed{8}$$

My mind is always going. I have ideas and ideas and more ideas. I have learned to capture these thoughts to clear my mind. David Allen, author of *Getting Things Done* says "In karate there is an image that's used to define the position of perfect readiness: 'mind like water.' Imagine throwing a pebble into a still pond. How does the water respond? The answer is, totally appropriately to the force and mass of the input; then it returns to calm. It doesn't overreact or underreact." If you can capture your free-flowing ideas, your mind can be clear to focus on your current project or to have more ideas.

There are so many great ways to capture ideas. You can use the old-school pen and notebook approach. My son has a hard time going to sleep at night as there are so many ideas in his head. He wants to be an inventor when he grows up, so he has a notebook to write down his invention ideas. This helps him quiet his thoughts so he can go to sleep — and you never know, someday those ideas might be worth millions. So might yours!

As I'm often on the go, I like to use the Evernote app to capture ideas that can be accessed from anywhere: on my phone, my work computer or my personal computer. I often use the voice to text feature on my phone to record my ideas right into Evernote. Here's another strategy when you're on the go... On my drive home from work, it's common that ideas pour into my head. I call myself (hands free of course) and leave myself a message for the next day. If you're not driving, you could also send an email to yourself to review the next day.

Whatever your method, it's especially important for introverts to record those never-ending ideas in some form, so you can get them out of your head concentrate on whatever needs your focus at the time.

For example, if I know I need to finish my section of a training by Friday, I need to make a note of when

I am going to do it and the steps I need to accomplish it. If I don't, my brain will keep bringing it up so that I don't forget. Having these to-do items bouncing around in my head prevents me from focusing on whatever I am supposed to be doing at the moment.

The capturing of my to-do's and my ideas has been extremely valuable to me. As an introvert, I naturally spend more of my time in my mind with my thoughts. I have so many great ideas, but I have to capture those ideas to make room for the new ideas to come. If I can keep my mind clear, I can focus on the task at hand and all the while continue to come up with great ideas for the future.

Ideally, the things I need to do will be captured as I go. However, when life gets a little busy, sometimes I need to step back and make sure that everything is recorded in an accessible place to make sure it will get done. As I make my plan for the week, I review those tasks and ideas that I have captured and incorporate them into my weekly schedule. Or I may just note them for future reference if they are not high priority.

Action steps:

1) When your mind is full of ideas, take time to capture those ideas so your mind can let them go or move on. Use pen/paper or a computer or phone app (like Evernote) to record your ideas.

2) If you're on the go, call or message yourself with important ideas and reminders so they'll be there waiting when you get back to your workspace.

3) Review your ideas and thoughts regularly, so you can incorporate what works and save ideas for future implementation if they're not for a current project.

Getting Organized

9

I've read numerous books on organization and productivity, and found some valuable information in some, but not as much in others. Organization is a critical part of productivity and time management. But as an introvert, I first had to understand myself and how I worked best before I could successfully implement organization tips or systems from others. Once you've come to understand your own strengths and needs, it becomes easier to tweak others' systems and ideas to work for your individual personality.

There are many products and apps to get organized. I have and will continue to experiment, but this book is not all about the technology that you should use. The technology to use is what works best for you. I am in favor of using as few systems as possible and want to be able to access my system anywhere online.

As far as getting organized, I have really benefited from David Allen's book, *Getting Things Done*. I enjoyed his ideas on productivity, and have incorporated many of these great suggestions to help myself "get things done." And because I know my strengths and needs as an introvert, I have been able to use his ideas on organizing workload to create a system that works really well for me.

I took the process outlined in Allen's book and used his criteria for dealing with "stuff" as he calls it, and applied it to my personal system. For example, using Allen's criteria when reviewing each item either on my to-do list or email, I decide if it is actionable. If no, then do one of the following: either trash it, add it to a someday/maybe list, or store it as reference material.

If it is actionable, then I need to decide if I should do it now. Allen has a rule that if it can be done in two minutes or less, then do it now. Or you can delegate it and put it on a waiting for list for later follow up. Or you can defer it and add it to a calendar with a next action for it.

As an introvert, email is usually my preferred method of communication. I can think before I respond and the record of the discussion can be retrieved later. So I have made Gmail my system for organizing not only my emails, but also a place to keep my tasks and projects all in one place that I can access wherever I have an Internet connection. I use my Google calendar to combine my tasks and calendar items within my one account.

I have created email folders adapted from the *Getting Things Done* (or GTD) system of "Someday," "To do," "To do today," "Follow up," and "Reference":

"Someday" – this is my email file for the good ideas, but are not a current priority.

"To do" – these are things I need to review, but are not urgent.

"To do today" – these are actionable items that must be done and I make a task item on my to-do list out of them with a deadline.

"Follow up" – these are for questions that I am waiting for a response to or something that I delegated that I need to follow up on.

"Reference" – these are emails that I am done with and are filed away for future reference. I used to make many more folders, but have found with an email program like Gmail, the search feature makes this unnecessary.

When it comes to keeping track of tasks, whether in my emails or not, I create the following calendar items:

To do today (one for each day)

Deadlines (one for each day)

To do this week (one for each week)

Someday (one that I move from week to week)

I can list what needs to be done on a particular day on the calendar item. Using the repeat feature. I create these items on the calendar for months or even years at a time. If you share your calendar with others, you can mark appointments (tasks) as "private" on your calendar. I do the same and make an appointment for "deadlines" on a particular day to keep me on track for projects and tasks. At the beginning of the day, I take some time to review these "to do today" items and make a plan for the day. I also will also review the "to do this week," "deadlines," and "someday" calendar items that I review at the end of each week to see if anything should be moved to a higher priority. I have found that having my emails and tasks in one place that are accessible on any

Today

7.00	to do / deadlines
8.00	weekly review/prep
9.00	new employee training
10.00	reflection time
11.00	new product meeting
12.00	lunch
1.00	appt. w/ Bob
2.00	conference planning
3.00	
4.00	
5.00	wrap up and review

I note my to-do list for the day/week at the top of my schedule so I can identify what projects I need to focus on.

Take time each day to prepare and plan.

Build in some quiet time after meetings

Leave some open time in your schedule to complete tasks and handle unforseen emergencies of my devices works well for me. Again, I think it is up to you the system you use, but the important thing is to be able to access your system wherever needed and to have everything in one place.

I've adopted ideas from many productivity experts to create workflow systems that work for me, but since everyone is different, you need to understand how you work best to create organizational systems that functions well for you. I will probably be forever tweaking my own systems, because I'm always thinking and looking for ways to improve and streamline my methods. And I always enjoy learning new ways of organizing and figuring out how to make systems work to my own strengths.

As mentioned in a previous chapter, I try to limit my distractions while focusing on specific projects, so I try to check email and run this process just a few times each day. If I am looking at my email all day long with a new one popping in every few minutes, I will never get anything done. I also want to make sure that I process my email regularly so I don't miss anything urgent that needs my attention.

Be Adaptable

Don't schedule your day too tightly. Every day is bound to have unexpected things occur. Some days there are fires to put out or often it is an important time to make connections. In his book *TouchPoints*, Doug Conant challenges readers to consider some interruptions as opportunities. I first heard of Conant as I was listening to the radio on the way home from work and my ears perked up as I heard him speak about this book that he co-authored with Mette Norgaard. Conant described himself as an introvert on this radio program, which of course grabbed my attention. Conant has had many, many years of high level leadership positions, including former president, CEO, and director of the Campbell Soup Company, among multiple others.

I heard Conant on this radio show talk about being "tough-minded with standards" and "tender-hearted with people." This describes me well. I do have tough standards, but one of my introvert abilities is to see the unique strengths in others as well as their weaknesses. Being able to see this in people helps me to be more patient and understanding as people strive to be their best, and also enables me to help them work within their strengths.

Of course, after hearing this interview, I ran right out and picked up a copy of *TouchPoints*, which I started reading immediately. In this book, Conant and Norgaard discuss how leaders are constantly faced with interruptions and have a choice how to view these interruptions. The authors describe these TouchPoints – the contacts we have with others – as follows:

"Every TouchPoint is spring-loaded with possibilities. Each one can build – or break – a relationship. Even a brief interaction can change the way people think about themselves, their leaders, and their future."

Soon after reading the book I had a day where I experienced several interruptions. In the midst of that very busy day, I certainly could have done without the intrusions. But I chose to see these as opportunities and tried to see how I could help those that were coming to me. I did not finish everything I had planned to do that day, but I think taking the time to foster these relationships was well worth it.

Interruptions are a part of every day work and life. Making the choice to view these as opportunities to strengthen relationships instead of seeing them as intrusions or impediments to your success can help you improve not just yourself, but your team and completely change your environment for the better.

Action Steps:

1) Identify areas where better organization skills might improve your workflow.

2) Understand your own strengths and weaknesses as you implement strategies to improve your workflow and organizational systems.

3) Find products or apps that will capture your tasks and projects all in one place.

4) Regularly review your to-do items and determine whether they should be done today, at a later date, delegated to someone else, or saved for some time in the future.

5) Regularly review your deadlines.

6) Do a weekly review of non-urgent tasks and items that you have marked as "someday."

7) As an introvert, approach problems and people with patience and understanding. Start seeing interactions and interruptions as opportunities to build relationships and connections, rather than seeing them as roadblocks keeping you from accomplishing your tasks.

Preparing
For Your Week

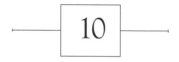

"Chance favors the prepared mind."
– Louis Pasteur

I believe that one of the keys to strength as an introvert is preparation. An introvert goes deep in thought and, given time, can come up with some brilliant ideas. That is not to say that we cannot come up with great ideas on the fly, because we can. I just know from experience that some of my best ideas have come with some time to think, while maybe scribbling some ideas on paper or typing them out on my computer. Or I may need to research a particular topic to gather as much information as possible. This goes for many things such as presentations, meetings, or projects. I do my best work when I can think ahead of time. Near the end of the week, I look ahead to the next week or so and review what is coming. I review my tasks and projects to see what are the most important priorities. For each upcoming activity or meeting, I see if I am prepared or if more preparation is needed and find time in my schedule to prepare.

A while back, I was giving an important presentation to a group of people that I had not spoken to before. Given this specific audience, I could not help but think that if I did a good job this could be a start of an ongoing presentation opportunity that I would welcome. However, the worrier in me kept thinking if the presentation were poor, this would be a one-time presentation, and I'd lose my chance to present to them again in the future.

I took a few minutes and did a little brainstorming with myself on a piece of paper to consider the needs of the audience. I kept that paper handy while I did some other work, and as ideas about this presentation continued to come, I made note of them. Once I had gathered all the topics that I wanted to share, I put them together in my presentation. The presentation went well because I had taken the extra time to prepare. As a result, I continue to present to this group and keep building a good relationship with them.

You may be jealous of those that can "wing it" in various situations. Don't be. They have their own strengths and you have yours. As an introvert, you have the ability to think deeply, make connections, and come up with some great ideas. This can be hard work, but of course success in any endeavor is hard work. "Chance" as it says above, or phrased another way, opportunities come to those who are prepared. What does it take for you to prepare?

I attend many meetings every day. Sometimes they are back-to-back for the entire day. It's a little frustrating as typically I am getting more and more projects and activities to do at these meetings and not getting any work done because of the meetings. In order to make sure my time spent at these meetings is productive, I have found that preparation is important.

Before the Meeting

I definitely like to give things some thought, so I make sure that I have the agenda ahead of time (and that there is an agenda). I may want to do some reading or do some research on the topic. If I'm in charge of the meeting, I try to send out the agenda in advance. If

I'm an attendee, I contact the person in charge to get a copy of the agenda prior to the meeting, so I have time to go over it. Also keep in mind that the more people in the meeting, the harder it may be to get all the points covered that you want to make. I write down points or questions that I feel need to be covered and bring this with me to the meeting.

During the Meeting

While the discussions are taking place, the conversations often spark ideas – sometimes related to the meeting topic and sometimes not. As these ideas come to me during the meeting I make sure to make note of them. This way, I have a list I can bring up either at an appropriate time during the meeting or cover at a later time. And sometimes I need to take time to think about things. I do my best work when I have gathered as much information as possible and then mull it over for awhile. I don't always need this processing time, but I do now give myself permission to ask the group that is meeting for "time to think." Some people may be impatient with having to wait for an answer, but just assure them this is how you work best and it is worth the wait. Sometimes you need to let others know how you work best.

After the Meeting

When I am back in my office, I take a few minutes to go through my notes from the meeting and am sure to capture those ideas, tasks, etc.

I also want to meet as needed and not more. Most calendars, such as those in Google or other places, are usually set up in half hour increments. One thing that drives me crazy is when people feel obligated to take the full amount of whatever meeting time was scheduled. Usually my approach is to get to the purpose of the meeting and then end when you end. The other day I had an hour-long meeting, but we got right down to business and finished in 15 minutes. I was conducting interviews after this meeting and it was nice to have some extra time to get set up and also relax for a minute. As an introvert, a little down time here and there is needed, but I don't always have it.

One thing we can do to keep meetings from running long is to cut down on excessive chit-chat and focus on the business at hand. Some chit-chat is critical to building relationships, so we need to be sure to include a bit of casual conversation. But when the casual conversation gets the meeting off-topic and starts wasting time, we need to gently bring attendees back to the agenda. This way, we take only the time we need to meet. Don't feel required to spend extra time just because you scheduled 30 minutes, if you only needed 17.

Preparation for projects is also important. I have learned that deadlines are very helpful to me as there is a time to think and a time to get things done. Not all introverts work well under deadlines, but I actually do better when I have a timeline that must be met. However, I have to schedule that critical time to think – ahead of time – in order to do my best work when it's actually time to do the work.

If you have a deadline coming up and need help with the "thinking" part of your project, here are a few ideas that might be helpful:

1) Understand that you need to allow yourself time to think about the project – this is especially important for introverts.

2) Set an appointment with yourself to ensure adequate thinking time – setting an appointment with yourself, like you would with anyone else, will ensure that can carve time out of your busy day to spend on the project.

3) Preparation is key – those brilliant ideas will come, but they require research, preparation and time.

4) Capture your ideas – if you have thoughts or ideas

that come to you about a certain project while you're working on something else, capture them so you can clear your mind to focus on the task at hand (and have that great idea handy when you need it!)

Knowing that I need time to think about a given project is half the battle. I do best with preparation, and after I prepare, I need to allow time for those ideas to roll around in my head. I need to make sure to carve out that needed time to prepare and think. As you're working on your next project or deadline, don't forget to plan your reflection time!

With time to reflect, an introvert can come up with some brilliant ideas. Have you ever felt like your mind was on fire? Or that thoughts were coming at you so fast and connections forming that you could hardly keep track of them?

I woke up early one morning with a problem on my mind... a very complex problem. A problem that I was giving myself time to think about. I really could not go back to sleep so I decided to head into work early. As I drove into work, I felt like my mind was "on fire." So many thoughts were coming into my head and the pieces of the problem were just falling into place. And on this day, as new ideas were coming into my head, I envisioned an innovative solution that would not require any additional resources. I got into work and immediately started writing down these ideas and mapping them out. It was amazing how it came together for me all at once — I developed a brilliant solution to this problem that I had chosen not to make a snap decision about.

Sometimes I make quick decisions and come up with quick solutions. But often, my best ideas and solutions to more complex issues come with time. The answers come by keeping the thoughts in the back of my mind and letting them roll around in my head for a while. I also do best when I have all of the information I can possibly can gather. A great strength of mine is gathering information and putting it together into innovative solutions. Sometimes when I'm trying to solve a problem, I need to remind myself to be patient, that good things — and good ideas — will come.

While I don't always have the luxury of taking time to solve a problem, nor can I always count on having a brilliant solution come to me on demand, experiencing the rush as my mind whirls to connect all the pieces is really quite remarkable. I know having to wait for an answer can drive people crazy when they are hoping for a quick solution, so I may need to ask for a little time to think. I let them know when I will get back to them and then come up with some good ideas.

Action Steps:

1) Make time each week to prepare for activities, meetings and presentations. Gather your information and thoughts ahead of time, so you are able to articulate your message and convey important points to others.

2) Prepare for projects and establish a timeline to be sure you meet your goals and deadlines. Remember there is a time to think and a time to do, and be sure to schedule time for both.

Be Strong!

I truly believe there is greatness in all of us. We just need to be reminded of this... sometimes over and over again. You have amazing gifts! Continue to learn about what makes you special. And don't listen to the any discouraging voices. We are not meant to just get by or survive. We are meant to THRIVE!

Introverts think deeply and often. You probably have many great ideas, some you have shared and perhaps some you have not. Within you are those thoughts and ideas that can greatly improve your own situation, make positive changes for those you care about, and perhaps impact society in general. Your gift is one of thinking and perhaps seeing things differently. Remember, your unique perspective of seeing differently is what it takes to make the world better.

If you are struggling, hang in there! I have learned over and over again that growth and progression come out of the struggle and I could share many examples. The content of this book is just one example of how struggle has created growth: Over the years, I've really learned how to best utilize my time. As my work and other responsibilities have increased, I have studied various time management strategies to be able to accomplish more and more with the same (or sometimes less) resources and time. However, just when I think I am really getting all the things done that I need to do, I get more to do! Through this struggle, I have become so much better at prioritizing and accomplishing the tasks I have been charged with.

Success is hard work. The key for introverts is not just working hard, but understanding how to harness the power of your incredible mind. You are a gifted thinker. You need time to clear your mind, prepare, reflect, and think. Taking a little time to plan and prepare will help you focus on your projects and work more efficiently. Recognizing when you need to recharge and allowing yourself some quiet time to reflect inwardly is necessary to keep you sharp and energetic throughout your day. Understanding and taking care of your introverted needs will allow your mind to function most effectively and become a powerful tool in your success.

What is most important to you? Set your priorities so you do and become what is most important. Approach life boldly with your introverted strengths and gifts and take care of your introverted needs while you are minding your time.

Recommended Reading

Below, find some of my favorite books on the subject of introversion, strengths, and time management.

Brain Rules by John J. Medina

Fearless by Steve Chandler

Getting Things Done by David Allen

Introvert Power by Laurie Helgoe

Linchpin by Seth Godin

Networking For People Who Hate Networking by Devora Zack

Now Discover Your Strengths by Marcus Buckingham and Donald Clifton

Off Balance by Matthew Kelley

Quiet by Susan Cain

Please Understand Me II by David Keirsey

Procrastinate on Purpose by Rory Vaden

The Introvert Advantage by Marti Olsen Laney

The Introvert's Way by Sophia Dembling

The Secret Lives of Introverts by Jenn Granneman

TouchPoints by Doug Conant and Mette Norgaard

What To Do When There's Too Much To Do by Laura Stack

Note: The above list contains affiliate links, and by clicking on them to purchase, you support the continued development of QuietandStrong. We appreciate your continued support of our efforts.

Your Free Bonus

As a small token of thanks for buying this book, I'd like to offer a free bonus gift exclusive to my readers.

This action-packed pdf bonus, called the MYT **WORKBOOK - 9 Strategies For Better Time Management, Especially for Introverts,** is designed to help you work through our action steps one section at a time.

This printable workbook contains the action steps from each chapter in a fillable, step-by-step format to help you journal and take notes as you complete each activity.

You can download your free bonus here:

http://quietandstrong.com/MYTbonus

If you enjoyed this book or found it helpful in some way, please consider leaving a review on

AMAZON or GOODREADS

Made in the USA
Middletown, DE
01 December 2018